ROLL-A-PROMPT WRITING JOURNAL

MYSTERY EDITION

MELISSA BANCZAK

LISA MAHONEY

Melissa -
Smoochous to Mark

Lisa -
For David who makes me laugh every day (and who would kill me if I sent
him smoochous)

ABOUT THE AUTHORS

In another lifetime, Melissa Banczak was an editor, ghost writer and literary agent specializing in screenplays. She writes the June Nash Mystery series and has a podcast called Books Cubed where she interviews the indie authors you should be reading. Her favorite games involve dice.

In this lifetime, Lisa Mahoney is an award-winning short story writer, adjunct English professor, and most importantly a dreamer. She hides her secret happiness when the power goes out and the generator won't work and her family is forced to play board games with her. She has just completed her first novel.

WHY WE WROTE THIS BOOK

Writers have imaginations. We play the *what-if* and *I-wonder-whether* games that make many of the realists around us scrunch up their noses. But sometimes we get stuck and our imaginations need to find a side door or a backdoor or even a trapdoor—a new way in to our stories. Once in, there's no telling where our creativity will take us. But how do we find those hidden passageways and allay our *stuckness*?

Many depend on prompt books. We're no different yet we yearned to have a *different approach*. So in our efforts to jumpstart our own writing and fire up our fantasies, we turned to our love of games and the randomness of dice and the Roll-A-Prompt Journal Series was born.

Use it alone or with friends. With over 6000 possible combinations, it's the perfect way to get your creative juices flowing.

Melissa & Lisa

HOW TO USE THIS BOOK

Each Roll-A-Prompt Writing Journal features 30 sets of elements that, with the roll of a dice, will create over 6000 prompts per book. What you'll need:

- Pen or pencil
- Dice (or trace the pattern on the next page)
- Imagination

Every story has a Main Character (referred to here as the MC) who drives the action. Each prompt begins with your character roll. After that, you'll get 2 of these 5 elements:

Trait I Location I Object I Word I Scenario

Roll for each selection and then jot it all down at the top of a work page. Once you have your prompt, let your imagination run wild.

A *late woman* doesn't just have to be someone running behind. She could also be pregnant. Or dead.

A *pizza delivery driver* is not just a job designation. It's also a treasure trove of stuff. They'd probably have a car. A phone. Some pizza. Use what you want. It's your prompt.

The paperback has 5 journal sheets per set so you can start writing. The ebook version includes a downloadable PDF.

Want to get even more out of this book? Turn to a random page for your first element. Another for your second. A third for the last. Voila! A new prompt.

So roll your dice, get writing, and above all, have fun!

Melissa & Lisa

We'd love to know how the prompts worked out for you. Did you start a story? Finish one? Publish? Did you try this with your writing group? Email us at mel@melissabanczak.com

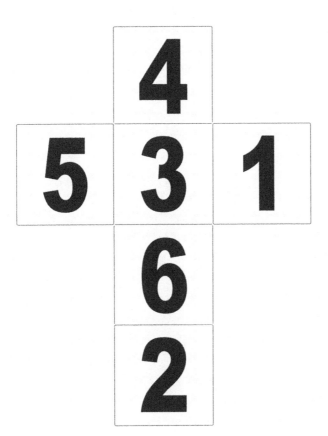

Character
Roll 1 Number

1. Airline pilot
2. Grandfather
3. Hip hop B-Boy
4. Zookeeper
5. Coach
6. Loan officer

Trait
Roll 1 Number

1. Studious
2. Lucky
3. Dramatic
4. Pouty
5. Giddy
6. Close talker

Location
Roll 1 Number

1. Bathtub
2. Dentist's wait room
3. Walking along train tracks
4. Strawberry patch
5. Rooftop pool
6. Stuck in an elevator

Character_____Trait_____
Location_____

_____
_____
_____
_____
_____
_____
_____
_____
_____
_____
_____
_____
_____
_____
_____
_____
_____
_____
_____
_____
_____
_____
_____
_____
_____
_____
_____
_____
_____
_____
_____
_____
_____
_____

Character_____Trait_____
Location_____

_____
_____
_____
_____
_____
_____
_____
_____
_____
_____
_____
_____
_____
_____
_____
_____
_____
_____
_____
_____
_____
_____
_____
_____
_____
_____
_____
_____
_____
_____
_____
_____
_____
_____
_____

Character_____Trait_____
Location_____

_____
_____
_____
_____
_____
_____
_____
_____
_____
_____
_____
_____
_____
_____
_____
_____
_____
_____
_____
_____
_____
_____
_____
_____
_____
_____
_____
_____
_____
_____
_____
_____
_____
_____

Character_____Trait_____
Location_____

_____
_____
_____
_____
_____
_____
_____
_____
_____
_____
_____
_____
_____
_____
_____
_____
_____
_____
_____
_____
_____
_____
_____
_____
_____
_____
_____
_____
_____
_____
_____
_____
_____
_____
_____

Character_____Trait_____
Location_____

_____
_____
_____
_____
_____
_____
_____
_____
_____
_____
_____
_____
_____
_____
_____
_____
_____
_____
_____
_____
_____
_____
_____
_____
_____
_____
_____
_____
_____
_____
_____
_____
_____
_____
_____
_____

STORY BUILDING

Character
Roll 1 Number

1. 17-year-old girl
2. Computer programmer
3. Gospel singer
4. Diner owner
5. Interior decorator
6. Sunbather

Object
Roll 1 Number

1. Fanny pack
2. Boutonniere
3. Rifle
4. Cotton ball
5. Yoga mat
6. Gum

Scenario
Roll 1 Number

1. Discovering a human bone
2. Binge watching a TV show
3. In a rainstorm
4. Setting up a campsite
5. Taking a museum tour
6. There's a safe house

Character _____Object_____

Scenario _____

_____
_____
_____
_____
_____
_____
_____
_____
_____
_____
_____
_____
_____
_____
_____
_____
_____
_____
_____
_____
_____
_____
_____
_____
_____
_____
_____
_____
_____
_____
_____
_____
_____
_____
_____
_____
_____
_____

Character _____ Object _____
Scenario _____

_____
_____
_____
_____
_____
_____
_____
_____
_____
_____
_____
_____
_____
_____
_____
_____
_____
_____
_____
_____
_____
_____
_____
_____
_____
_____
_____
_____
_____
_____
_____
_____
_____
_____
_____
_____
_____

Character _____Object_____

Scenario _____

_____
_____
_____
_____
_____
_____
_____
_____
_____
_____
_____
_____
_____
_____
_____
_____
_____
_____
_____
_____
_____
_____
_____
_____
_____
_____
_____
_____
_____
_____
_____
_____
_____

Character _____Object_____

Scenario _____

_____
_____
_____
_____
_____
_____
_____
_____
_____
_____
_____
_____
_____
_____
_____
_____
_____
_____
_____
_____
_____
_____
_____
_____
_____
_____
_____
_____
_____
_____
_____
_____
_____

Character _____Object_____

Scenario _____

_____

_____

_____

_____

_____

_____

_____

_____

_____

_____

_____

_____

_____

_____

_____

_____

_____

_____

_____

_____

_____

_____

_____

_____

_____

_____

_____

_____

_____

_____

_____

_____

_____

_____

Character
Roll 1 Number

1. College student
2. Midwife
3. Guitar player
4. Playwright
5. Sailor
6. Judge

Object
Roll 1 Number

1. Acorn
2. Coat hanger
3. Fake mustache
4. Salt shaker
5. Kite
6. Teabag

Word
Roll 1 Number

1. Injury
2. Vital
3. Absorb
4. Change
5. Elite
6. Locate

Character_____
Object _____Word _____

_____
_____
_____
_____
_____
_____
_____
_____
_____
_____
_____
_____
_____
_____
_____
_____
_____
_____
_____
_____
_____
_____
_____
_____
_____
_____
_____
_____
_____
_____
_____
_____

Character_____

Object _____Word _____

_____
_____
_____
_____
_____
_____
_____
_____
_____
_____
_____
_____
_____
_____
_____
_____
_____
_____
_____
_____
_____
_____
_____
_____
_____
_____
_____
_____
_____
_____
_____
_____
_____
_____
_____
_____

Character_____

Object _____Word _____

_____
_____
_____
_____
_____
_____
_____
_____
_____
_____
_____
_____
_____
_____
_____
_____
_____
_____
_____
_____
_____
_____
_____
_____
_____
_____
_____
_____
_____
_____
_____
_____

Character_____

Object _____Word _____

_____
_____
_____
_____
_____
_____
_____
_____
_____
_____
_____
_____
_____
_____
_____
_____
_____
_____
_____
_____
_____
_____
_____
_____
_____
_____
_____
_____
_____
_____
_____
_____
_____

Character_____

Object _____Word _____

_____
_____
_____
_____
_____
_____
_____
_____
_____
_____
_____
_____
_____
_____
_____
_____
_____
_____
_____
_____
_____
_____
_____
_____
_____
_____
_____
_____
_____
_____
_____
_____
_____
_____
_____

STORY BUILDING

Character
Roll 1 Number

1. Alligator wrestler
2. Guitarist
3. Seamstress
4. Typist
5. Watch maker
6. Math tutor

Word
Roll 1 Number

1. Less
2. Owl
3. Lightbulb
4. Memory
5. Skip
6. Bulbous

Scenario
Roll 1 Number

1. There's a fire
2. Giving a presentation
3. Taking a hike
4. Police lineup
5. Carwash at midnight
6. Rescuing a cat

Character_____Word_____
Scenario_____

_____
_____
_____
_____
_____
_____
_____
_____
_____
_____
_____
_____
_____
_____
_____
_____
_____
_____
_____
_____
_____
_____
_____
_____
_____
_____
_____
_____
_____
_____
_____
_____
_____
_____
_____
_____

Character_____Word_____

Scenario_____

_____
_____
_____
_____
_____
_____
_____
_____
_____
_____
_____
_____
_____
_____
_____
_____
_____
_____
_____
_____
_____
_____
_____
_____
_____
_____
_____
_____
_____
_____
_____
_____
_____
_____

Character_____Word_____
Scenario_____

_____
_____
_____
_____
_____
_____
_____
_____
_____
_____
_____
_____
_____
_____
_____
_____
_____
_____
_____
_____
_____
_____
_____
_____
_____
_____
_____
_____
_____
_____
_____
_____
_____
_____
_____
_____
_____
_____
_____
_____

Character_____Word_____
Scenario_____
_____
_____
_____
_____
_____
_____
_____
_____
_____
_____
_____
_____
_____
_____
_____
_____
_____
_____
_____
_____
_____
_____
_____
_____
_____
_____
_____
_____
_____
_____
_____
_____
_____
_____
_____
_____

Character_____Word_____
Scenario_____

_____
_____
_____
_____
_____
_____
_____
_____
_____
_____
_____
_____
_____
_____
_____
_____
_____
_____
_____
_____
_____
_____
_____
_____
_____
_____
_____
_____
_____
_____
_____
_____
_____
_____
_____

Character
Roll 1 Number

1. Donut maker on the night shift
2. Magician about to perform
3. 8-year-old boy who can't sleep
4. Boater on a glassy ocean
5. Street sweeper on a crowded road
6. Marriage therapist between patients

Mood
Roll 1 Number

1. Happy
2. Whimsical
3. Reflective
4. Feeble
5. Tense
6. Gloomy

Word
Roll 1 Number

1. Spirit
2. Buoyant
3. Vile
4. Reaction
5. Cold
6. Hair

Character_____

Mood_____Word _____

Character_____

Mood_____Word_____

Character_____

Mood_____Word _____

_____
_____
_____
_____
_____
_____
_____
_____
_____
_____
_____
_____
_____
_____
_____
_____
_____
_____
_____
_____
_____
_____
_____
_____
_____
_____
_____
_____
_____
_____
_____
_____
_____
_____
_____

Character_____

Mood_____Word _____

Character_____

Mood_____Word _____

_____
_____
_____
_____
_____
_____
_____
_____
_____
_____
_____
_____
_____
_____
_____
_____
_____
_____
_____
_____
_____
_____
_____
_____
_____
_____
_____
_____
_____
_____
_____
_____

STORY BUILDING

Character
Roll 1 number
Even = MC is alone
Odd = Roll again for a companion

1. Deaf interpreter
2. Insomniac
3. Medical examiner
4. 50-year-old man
5. AA sponsor
6. Stunt driver

IF the MC is alone, add an object
Roll 1 Number

1. Mouth guard
2. Red rose
3. Kitchen sponge
4. Glasses
5. Cowboy hat
6. Barbell

Scenario
Roll 1 Number

1. Interrupting a thief
2. Pick-up game of basketball
3. Run off the road
4. House breaker trips
5. Early morning lap pool
6. Four cars at a 4-way stop

Character(s)_____

Object_____

Scenario_____

_____
_____
_____
_____
_____
_____
_____
_____
_____
_____
_____
_____
_____
_____
_____
_____
_____
_____
_____
_____
_____
_____
_____
_____
_____
_____
_____
_____
_____
_____
_____
_____
_____
_____

Character(s)_____

Object_____

Scenario_____

Character(s)_____

Object_____

Scenario_____

_____
_____
_____
_____
_____
_____
_____
_____
_____
_____
_____
_____
_____
_____
_____
_____
_____
_____
_____
_____
_____
_____
_____
_____
_____
_____
_____
_____
_____
_____
_____
_____
_____
_____
_____
_____
_____

Character(s)_____

Object_____

Scenario_____

Character(s)_____

Object_____

Scenario_____

_____
_____
_____
_____
_____
_____
_____
_____
_____
_____
_____
_____
_____
_____
_____
_____
_____
_____
_____
_____
_____
_____
_____
_____
_____
_____
_____
_____
_____
_____
_____
_____
_____
_____
_____
_____

STORY BUILDING

Character
Roll 1 Number

1. Salsa dancer
2. Mistress
3. Nun
4. Victim advocate
5. Pig farmer
6. Tech support

Trait
Roll 1 Number

1. Hyperactive
2. Idyllic
3. Regal
4. Giggly
5. Worried
6. Comfortable

Location
Roll 1 Number

1. Outhouse
2. Swimming quarry
3. Attic
4. Riding a carousel
5. Firehouse
6. Industrial kitchen

Character_____Trait_____
Location_____

_____
_____
_____
_____
_____
_____
_____
_____
_____
_____
_____
_____
_____
_____
_____
_____
_____
_____
_____
_____
_____
_____
_____
_____
_____
_____
_____
_____
_____
_____
_____
_____
_____
_____
_____
_____

Character_____Trait_____
Location_____

_____
_____
_____
_____
_____
_____
_____
_____
_____
_____
_____
_____
_____
_____
_____
_____
_____
_____
_____
_____
_____
_____
_____
_____
_____
_____
_____
_____
_____
_____
_____
_____
_____
_____

Character_____Trait_____
Location_____

_____
_____
_____
_____
_____
_____
_____
_____
_____
_____
_____
_____
_____
_____
_____
_____
_____
_____
_____
_____
_____
_____
_____
_____
_____
_____
_____
_____
_____
_____
_____
_____
_____
_____
_____

Character_____Trait_____
Location_____

_____
_____
_____
_____
_____
_____
_____
_____
_____
_____
_____
_____
_____
_____
_____
_____
_____
_____
_____
_____
_____
_____
_____
_____
_____
_____
_____
_____
_____
_____
_____
_____
_____
_____
_____
_____
_____
_____
_____

Character_____Trait_____
Location_____

_____
_____
_____
_____
_____
_____
_____
_____
_____
_____
_____
_____
_____
_____
_____
_____
_____
_____
_____
_____
_____
_____
_____
_____
_____
_____
_____
_____
_____
_____
_____
_____

STORY BUILDING

Character
Roll 1 Number

1. Daycare owner
2. Fingerprint specialist
3. Health inspector
4. Graffiti artist
5. Stunt driver
6. Magician

Object
Roll 1 Number

1. Scrapbook
2. 10 lb bag of potatoes
3. Mask
4. Rake
5. Piano
6. Eye patch

Scenario
Roll 1 Number

1. Engaged in a barroom fight
2. Unsigned letter is delivered
3. Map without labels discovered in a hidden drawer
4. Surveillance van on a stakeout
5. Mercy meal (potluck after wake)
6. Inside a jury deliberation room

Character_____Object_____

Scenario_____

_____
_____
_____
_____
_____
_____
_____
_____
_____
_____
_____
_____
_____
_____
_____
_____
_____
_____
_____
_____
_____
_____
_____
_____
_____
_____
_____
_____
_____
_____
_____
_____
_____
_____
_____
_____

Character_____Object_____
Scenario_____

_____
_____
_____
_____
_____
_____
_____
_____
_____
_____
_____
_____
_____
_____
_____
_____
_____
_____
_____
_____
_____
_____
_____
_____
_____
_____
_____
_____
_____
_____
_____
_____
_____
_____
_____
_____
_____
_____

Character_____Object_____
Scenario_____

_____
_____
_____
_____
_____
_____
_____
_____
_____
_____
_____
_____
_____
_____
_____
_____
_____
_____
_____
_____
_____
_____
_____
_____
_____
_____
_____
_____
_____
_____
_____
_____
_____
_____
_____
_____
_____

Character_____Object_____
Scenario_____

_____
_____
_____
_____
_____
_____
_____
_____
_____
_____
_____
_____
_____
_____
_____
_____
_____
_____
_____
_____
_____
_____
_____
_____
_____
_____
_____
_____
_____
_____
_____
_____
_____
_____
_____

Character_____Object_____

Scenario_____

_____

_____

_____

_____

_____

_____

_____

_____

_____

_____

_____

_____

_____

_____

_____

_____

_____

_____

_____

_____

_____

_____

_____

_____

_____

_____

_____

_____

_____

_____

_____

_____

_____

_____

_____

_____

_____

CHARACTER BUILDING

Character
Roll 1 Number

1. Snowplow driver
2. Pharmacist
3. Boxer
4. Foreign exchange student
5. Assistant DA
6. Housewife

Object
Roll 1 Number

1. Adirondack chair
2. Flashlight
3. Empty pizza box
4. Rusty razorblade
5. Earring back
6. Bathroom scale

Word
Roll 1 Number

1. Alibi
2. Change
3. Hang-up
4. Push
5. Nonstop
6. Scuff

Character_____

Object _____Word _____

Character_____

Object _____Word _____

_____
_____
_____
_____
_____
_____
_____
_____
_____
_____
_____
_____
_____
_____
_____
_____
_____
_____
_____
_____
_____
_____
_____
_____
_____
_____
_____
_____
_____
_____
_____
_____
_____
_____
_____
_____

Character_____

Object _____Word _____

_____
_____
_____
_____
_____
_____
_____
_____
_____
_____
_____
_____
_____
_____
_____
_____
_____
_____
_____
_____
_____
_____
_____
_____
_____
_____
_____
_____
_____
_____
_____
_____
_____
_____
_____

Character_____

Object _____Word _____

Character_____

Object _____Word _____

_____
_____
_____
_____
_____
_____
_____
_____
_____
_____
_____
_____
_____
_____
_____
_____
_____
_____
_____
_____
_____
_____
_____
_____
_____
_____
_____
_____
_____
_____
_____
_____
_____
_____
_____
_____
_____

STORY BUILDING

Character
Roll 1 Number

1. CDC employee
2. Youth chorus singer
3. Hitchhiking hippie
4. Beekeeper
5. K9 officer
6. Stepmother

Word
Roll 1 Number

1. Guilty
2. Ease
3. Quit
4. Memory
5. Scowl
6. Background

Scenario
Roll 1 Number

1. Arguing with a bully
2. Receiving a phone call at 2 am
3. Serving as a jury foreman
4. Walking down an alley
5. Photographs arrive in the mail
6. Dog with a note tucked in his collar

Character_____Word_____
Scenario_____

_____
_____
_____
_____
_____
_____
_____
_____
_____
_____
_____
_____
_____
_____
_____
_____
_____
_____
_____
_____
_____
_____
_____
_____
_____
_____
_____
_____
_____
_____
_____
_____
_____
_____
_____
_____
_____

Character_____Word_____
Scenario_____

_____
_____
_____
_____
_____
_____
_____
_____
_____
_____
_____
_____
_____
_____
_____
_____
_____
_____
_____
_____
_____
_____
_____
_____
_____
_____
_____
_____
_____
_____
_____
_____
_____

Character_____Word_____

Scenario_____

_____

_____

_____

_____

_____

_____

_____

_____

_____

_____

_____

_____

_____

_____

_____

_____

_____

_____

_____

_____

_____

_____

_____

_____

_____

_____

_____

_____

_____

_____

_____

_____

_____

_____

_____

_____

_____

_____

Character_____Word_____
Scenario_____

_____
_____
_____
_____
_____
_____
_____
_____
_____
_____
_____
_____
_____
_____
_____
_____
_____
_____
_____
_____
_____
_____
_____
_____
_____
_____
_____
_____
_____
_____
_____
_____
_____
_____
_____
_____
_____
_____

Character_____Word_____

Scenario_____

_____
_____
_____
_____
_____
_____
_____
_____
_____
_____
_____
_____
_____
_____
_____
_____
_____
_____
_____
_____
_____
_____
_____
_____
_____
_____
_____
_____
_____
_____
_____
_____
_____
_____
_____
_____
_____

CHARACTER BUILDING

Character
Roll 1 Number

1. 19-year-old frat boy
2. League axe thrower
3. Kidnapper
4. Big sister
5. Hotel maid
6. Variety show contestant

Mood
Roll 1 Number

1. Hopeful
2. Complacent
3. Suspicious
4. Invisible
5. Frustrated
6. Quiet

Word
Roll 1 Number

1. Accomplice
2. Yellow
3. DNA
4. Spin
5. Repair
6. Boilerplate

Character_____

Mood_____Word _____

Character_____

Mood_____Word _____

_____
_____
_____
_____
_____
_____
_____
_____
_____
_____
_____
_____
_____
_____
_____
_____
_____
_____
_____
_____
_____
_____
_____
_____
_____
_____
_____
_____
_____
_____
_____

Character_____

Mood_____Word _____

_____
_____
_____
_____
_____
_____
_____
_____
_____
_____
_____
_____
_____
_____
_____
_____
_____
_____
_____
_____
_____
_____
_____
_____
_____
_____
_____
_____
_____
_____
_____
_____
_____
_____

Character_____

Mood_____Word _____

_____
_____
_____
_____
_____
_____
_____
_____
_____
_____
_____
_____
_____
_____
_____
_____
_____
_____
_____
_____
_____
_____
_____
_____
_____
_____
_____
_____
_____
_____

Character_____

Mood_____Word _____

_____
_____
_____
_____
_____
_____
_____
_____
_____
_____
_____
_____
_____
_____
_____
_____
_____
_____
_____
_____
_____
_____
_____
_____
_____
_____
_____
_____
_____
_____
_____
_____
_____
_____
_____
_____
_____
_____

Character
Roll 1 number
Even = MC is alone
Odd = Roll again for a companion

1. Cigar-maker
2. Gymnastics coach
3. Lobster boat captain
4. Retail store clerk
5. Mall ear-piercing kiosk girl
6. Survivalist

IF the MC is alone, add an object
Roll 1 Number

1. Air conditioner
2. Exit sign
3. Crib
4. Quarter
5. Bulletproof vest
6. Desk calendar

Scenario
Roll 1 Number

1. Cleaning up a crime scene
2. Falling into a ravine
3. Motor won't start
4. Unclogging a stopped-up sink
5. Kids running through a broken fire hydrant
6. Developing film in a dark room

Character(s)_____

Object_____

Scenario_____

_____
_____
_____
_____
_____
_____
_____
_____
_____
_____
_____
_____
_____
_____
_____
_____
_____
_____
_____
_____
_____
_____
_____
_____
_____
_____
_____
_____
_____
_____
_____
_____

Character(s)_____
Object_____
Scenario_____

_____
_____
_____
_____
_____
_____
_____
_____
_____
_____
_____
_____
_____
_____
_____
_____
_____
_____
_____
_____
_____
_____
_____
_____
_____
_____
_____
_____
_____
_____
_____
_____
_____
_____
_____
_____
_____

Character(s)_____

Object_____

Scenario_____

_____
_____
_____
_____
_____
_____
_____
_____
_____
_____
_____
_____
_____
_____
_____
_____
_____
_____
_____
_____
_____
_____
_____
_____
_____
_____
_____
_____
_____
_____
_____

Character(s)_____

Object_____

Scenario_____

_____
_____
_____
_____
_____
_____
_____
_____
_____
_____
_____
_____
_____
_____
_____
_____
_____
_____
_____
_____
_____
_____
_____
_____
_____
_____
_____
_____
_____
_____
_____
_____
_____
_____

Character(s)_____

Object_____

Scenario_____

_____
_____
_____
_____
_____
_____
_____
_____
_____
_____
_____
_____
_____
_____
_____
_____
_____
_____
_____
_____
_____
_____
_____
_____
_____
_____
_____
_____
_____
_____
_____
_____
_____
_____
_____
_____

STORY BUILDING

Character
Roll 1 Number

1. Abused husband
2. Dog breeder
3. Cake decorator
4. Triathlete
5. Youtuber
6. State senator

Trait
Roll 1 Number

1. Altruistic
2. Sickly
3. Chirpy
4. Disobedient
5. Enigmatic
6. Proper

Location
Roll 1 Number

1. On a country lane
2. Behind a DJ booth at a nightclub
3. Hiding in a root cellar
4. Crowded elevator
5. Breakfast diner
6. High school chemistry lab

Character_____Trait_____
Location_____

_____
_____
_____
_____
_____
_____
_____
_____
_____
_____
_____
_____
_____
_____
_____
_____
_____
_____
_____
_____
_____
_____
_____
_____
_____
_____
_____
_____
_____
_____
_____
_____

Character_____Trait_____
Location_____

_____
_____
_____
_____
_____
_____
_____
_____
_____
_____
_____
_____
_____
_____
_____
_____
_____
_____
_____
_____
_____
_____
_____
_____
_____
_____
_____
_____
_____
_____
_____
_____
_____
_____

Character_____Trait_____
Location_____

_____
_____
_____
_____
_____
_____
_____
_____
_____
_____
_____
_____
_____
_____
_____
_____
_____
_____
_____
_____
_____
_____
_____
_____
_____
_____
_____
_____
_____
_____
_____
_____
_____
_____
_____
_____

Character_____Trait_____
Location_____

_____
_____
_____
_____
_____
_____
_____
_____
_____
_____
_____
_____
_____
_____
_____
_____
_____
_____
_____
_____
_____
_____
_____
_____
_____
_____
_____
_____
_____
_____
_____
_____
_____
_____
_____
_____

Character_____Trait_____
Location_____

_____
_____
_____
_____
_____
_____
_____
_____
_____
_____
_____
_____
_____
_____
_____
_____
_____
_____
_____
_____
_____
_____
_____
_____
_____
_____
_____
_____
_____
_____
_____
_____
_____
_____
_____
_____

Character
Roll 1 Number

1. International student from Barcelona
2. Computer repairman
3. Masseuse
4. Lifeguard
5. 40-year-old divorcee
6. Sign painter

Object
Roll 1 Number

1. Air freshener
2. Tape measure
3. Palm frond
4. Microwave oven
5. Pillow
6. File folder

Scenario
Roll 1 Number

1. Being interrogated by the police
2. Going through a carwash
3. Meeting with a professor about an assignment
4. Discovering a long lost family heirloom
5. Calling to make a sensitive doctor's appointment
6. Fixing a broken plank on a wooden deck

Character_____Object_____
Scenario_____

_____
_____
_____
_____
_____
_____
_____
_____
_____
_____
_____
_____
_____
_____
_____
_____
_____
_____
_____
_____
_____
_____
_____
_____
_____
_____
_____
_____
_____
_____
_____
_____

Character_____Object_____
Scenario_____

_____
_____
_____
_____
_____
_____
_____
_____
_____
_____
_____
_____
_____
_____
_____
_____
_____
_____
_____
_____
_____
_____
_____
_____
_____
_____
_____
_____
_____
_____
_____
_____
_____
_____
_____
_____
_____
_____

Character_____Object_____

Scenario_____

_____
_____
_____
_____
_____
_____
_____
_____
_____
_____
_____
_____
_____
_____
_____
_____
_____
_____
_____
_____
_____
_____
_____
_____
_____
_____
_____
_____
_____
_____
_____
_____

Character_____Object_____
Scenario_____

_____
_____
_____
_____
_____
_____
_____
_____
_____
_____
_____
_____
_____
_____
_____
_____
_____
_____
_____
_____
_____
_____
_____
_____
_____
_____
_____
_____
_____
_____
_____
_____
_____

Character_____Object_____
Scenario_____

_____
_____
_____
_____
_____
_____
_____
_____
_____
_____
_____
_____
_____
_____
_____
_____
_____
_____
_____
_____
_____
_____
_____
_____
_____
_____
_____
_____
_____
_____
_____
_____

Character
Roll 1 Number

1. Foster dad
2. Kindergarten teacher
3. Doll collector
4. Olympic runner
5. Russian translator
6. Puppeteer

Object
Roll 1 Number

1. Antibacterial soap
2. Lazy Susan
3. Crime scene tape
4. Ballet slipper
5. Stop sign
6. Gas grill

Word
Roll 1 Number

1. Greed
2. Stream
3. Identify
4. Certified
5. Refuse
6. Free

Character_____

Object _____Word _____

_____
_____
_____
_____
_____
_____
_____
_____
_____
_____
_____
_____
_____
_____
_____
_____
_____
_____
_____
_____
_____
_____
_____
_____
_____
_____
_____
_____
_____
_____
_____
_____
_____
_____

Character_____

Object _____Word _____

_____
_____
_____
_____
_____
_____
_____
_____
_____
_____
_____
_____
_____
_____
_____
_____
_____
_____
_____
_____
_____
_____
_____
_____
_____
_____
_____
_____
_____
_____
_____
_____
_____

Character_____

Object _____Word _____

_____
_____
_____
_____
_____
_____
_____
_____
_____
_____
_____
_____
_____
_____
_____
_____
_____
_____
_____
_____
_____
_____
_____
_____
_____
_____
_____
_____
_____
_____
_____
_____
_____

Character_____

Object _____Word _____

Character_____

Object _____Word _____

_____
_____
_____
_____
_____
_____
_____
_____
_____
_____
_____
_____
_____
_____
_____
_____
_____
_____
_____
_____
_____
_____
_____
_____
_____
_____
_____
_____
_____
_____
_____
_____
_____

STORY BUILDING

Character
Roll 1 Number

1. Crossing guard
2. Gambler
3. Wedding planner
4. Professional mover
5. Gunslinger re-enactor
6. 8-year-old class clown

Word
Roll 1 Number

1. Fugitive
2. Impact
3. Possess
4. Video
5. Wrong
6. Novel

Scenario
Roll 1 Number

1. Escaping from a house fire
2. Escorting a donated organ
3. Sneaking into a movie theater
4. Placing a bet at the horse race
5. Conducting an autopsy
6. Getting a pedicure

Character_____Word_____
Scenario_____

_____
_____
_____
_____
_____
_____
_____
_____
_____
_____
_____
_____
_____
_____
_____
_____
_____
_____
_____
_____
_____
_____
_____
_____
_____
_____
_____
_____
_____
_____
_____
_____

Character_____Word_____
Scenario_____

_____
_____
_____
_____
_____
_____
_____
_____
_____
_____
_____
_____
_____
_____
_____
_____
_____
_____
_____
_____
_____
_____
_____
_____
_____
_____
_____
_____
_____
_____
_____
_____
_____
_____

Character_____Word_____
Scenario_____

_____
_____
_____
_____
_____
_____
_____
_____
_____
_____
_____
_____
_____
_____
_____
_____
_____
_____
_____
_____
_____
_____
_____
_____
_____
_____
_____
_____
_____
_____
_____
_____
_____
_____
_____

Character_____Word_____
Scenario_____

_____
_____
_____
_____
_____
_____
_____
_____
_____
_____
_____
_____
_____
_____
_____
_____
_____
_____
_____
_____
_____
_____
_____
_____
_____
_____
_____
_____
_____
_____
_____
_____

Character_____Word_____
Scenario_____

_____
_____
_____
_____
_____
_____
_____
_____
_____
_____
_____
_____
_____
_____
_____
_____
_____
_____
_____
_____
_____
_____
_____
_____
_____
_____
_____
_____
_____
_____
_____
_____
_____
_____

Character
Roll 1 Number

1. Jeweler
2. Teenage babysitter
3. Lounge singer
4. Book binder
5. Philosophy professor
6. Exercise instructor

Mood
Roll 1 Number

1. Sad
2. Celebratory
3. Jealous
4. Frenetic
5. Exhilarated
6. Apathetic

Word
Roll 1 Number

1. Hair
2. Justice
3. Encounter
4. Trusted
5. Angle
6. Remains

Character_____

Mood_____Word _____

_____
_____
_____
_____
_____
_____
_____
_____
_____
_____
_____
_____
_____
_____
_____
_____
_____
_____
_____
_____
_____
_____
_____
_____
_____
_____
_____
_____
_____
_____
_____
_____
_____

Character_____

Mood_____Word _____

_____
_____
_____
_____
_____
_____
_____
_____
_____
_____
_____
_____
_____
_____
_____
_____
_____
_____
_____
_____
_____
_____
_____
_____
_____
_____
_____
_____
_____

Character_____

Mood_____Word _____

Character_____

Mood_____Word _____

_____
_____
_____
_____
_____
_____
_____
_____
_____
_____
_____
_____
_____
_____
_____
_____
_____
_____
_____
_____
_____
_____
_____
_____
_____
_____
_____
_____
_____
_____
_____
_____
_____
_____
_____
_____
_____

Character_____
Mood_____Word _____

_____
_____
_____
_____
_____
_____
_____
_____
_____
_____
_____
_____
_____
_____
_____
_____
_____
_____
_____
_____
_____
_____
_____
_____
_____
_____
_____
_____
_____
_____
_____
_____
_____
_____
_____
_____
_____
_____

Character
Roll 1 number
Even = MC is alone
Odd = Roll again for a companion

1. Serial killer
2. Makeup artist
3. Drummer in a marching band
4. AC repairman
5. Flight attendant
6. Chancellor of a university

IF the MC is alone, add an object
Roll 1 Number

1. Canoe
2. Bullet casing
3. Hanger
4. Apple corer
5. Gun
6. Dice

Scenario
Roll 1 Number

1. On a stakeout
2. Walking through a cemetery at night
3. Bike gets a flat tire
4. Consenting to a medical trial
5. Noticing a man with a gun entering a store
6. Watching TV at 3:00 am

Character(s)_____

Object_____

Scenario_____

Character(s)_____

Object_____

Scenario_____

_____
_____
_____
_____
_____
_____
_____
_____
_____
_____
_____
_____
_____
_____
_____
_____
_____
_____
_____
_____
_____
_____
_____
_____
_____
_____
_____
_____
_____
_____
_____
_____
_____

Character(s)_____

Object_____

Scenario_____

_____
_____
_____
_____
_____
_____
_____
_____
_____
_____
_____
_____
_____
_____
_____
_____
_____
_____
_____
_____
_____
_____
_____
_____
_____
_____
_____
_____
_____
_____
_____
_____
_____
_____
_____
_____
_____

Character(s)_____

Object_____

Scenario_____

_____
_____
_____
_____
_____
_____
_____
_____
_____
_____
_____
_____
_____
_____
_____
_____
_____
_____
_____
_____
_____
_____
_____
_____
_____
_____
_____
_____
_____
_____
_____
_____

Character(s)_____

Object_____

Scenario_____

_____
_____
_____
_____
_____
_____
_____
_____
_____
_____
_____
_____
_____
_____
_____
_____
_____
_____
_____
_____
_____
_____
_____
_____
_____
_____
_____
_____
_____
_____
_____
_____

STORY BUILDING

Character
Roll 1 Number

1. Justice of the peace
2. Carpet cleaner
3. Bootlegger
4. Horse trainer
5. Sumo wrestler
6. Restaurant host/hostess

Trait
Roll 1 Number

1. Intuitive
2. Lucky
3. Muscle-head
4. Nervous
5. Demure
6. Flighty

Location
Roll 1 Number

1. Garage
2. Woodworking shop
3. In line at a bank
4. Apple orchard
5. Sitting in a sauna
6. In the bed of an 18-wheeler

Character_____Trait_____
Location_____

_____
_____
_____
_____
_____
_____
_____
_____
_____
_____
_____
_____
_____
_____
_____
_____
_____
_____
_____
_____
_____
_____
_____
_____
_____
_____
_____
_____
_____
_____
_____
_____
_____
_____
_____
_____
_____

Character_____Trait_____
Location_____

_____
_____
_____
_____
_____
_____
_____
_____
_____
_____
_____
_____
_____
_____
_____
_____
_____
_____
_____
_____
_____
_____
_____
_____
_____
_____
_____
_____
_____
_____
_____
_____
_____
_____

Character_____Trait_____
Location_____

_____
_____
_____
_____
_____
_____
_____
_____
_____
_____
_____
_____
_____
_____
_____
_____
_____
_____
_____
_____
_____
_____
_____
_____
_____
_____
_____
_____
_____
_____
_____
_____
_____

Character_____Trait_____
Location_____

_____
_____
_____
_____
_____
_____
_____
_____
_____
_____
_____
_____
_____
_____
_____
_____
_____
_____
_____
_____
_____
_____
_____
_____
_____
_____
_____
_____
_____
_____
_____
_____
_____
_____

Character_____Trait_____
Location_____

_____
_____
_____
_____
_____
_____
_____
_____
_____
_____
_____
_____
_____
_____
_____
_____
_____
_____
_____
_____
_____
_____
_____
_____
_____
_____
_____
_____
_____
_____
_____
_____
_____
_____
_____

STORY BUILDING

Character
Roll 1 Number

1. Custodian
2. Karate instructor
3. House flipper
4. Bank cashier
5. Alcoholic
6. Mother-in-law

Object
Roll 1 Number

1. American flag
2. Card table
3. Jack-o-lantern
4. Paper plate
5. Hair ribbon
6. Blender

Scenario
Roll 1 Number

1. Watching surveillance tapes
2. Something is stuck in the garbage disposal
3. Car on the side of the road on fire
4. Abandoned cart at the supermarket
5. Man at a nearby table collapses
6. Passenger is late for a private flight

Character_____Object_____

Scenario_____

_____

_____

_____

_____

_____

_____

_____

_____

_____

_____

_____

_____

_____

_____

_____

_____

_____

_____

_____

_____

_____

_____

_____

_____

_____

_____

_____

_____

_____

_____

_____

_____

Character_____Object_____
Scenario_____

_____
_____
_____
_____
_____
_____
_____
_____
_____
_____
_____
_____
_____
_____
_____
_____
_____
_____
_____
_____
_____
_____
_____
_____
_____
_____
_____
_____
_____
_____
_____
_____
_____
_____
_____
_____

Character_____Object_____
Scenario_____

_____
_____
_____
_____
_____
_____
_____
_____
_____
_____
_____
_____
_____
_____
_____
_____
_____
_____
_____
_____
_____
_____
_____
_____
_____
_____
_____
_____
_____
_____
_____
_____
_____
_____
_____
_____

Character_____Object_____

Scenario_____

_____
_____
_____
_____
_____
_____
_____
_____
_____
_____
_____
_____
_____
_____
_____
_____
_____
_____
_____
_____
_____
_____
_____
_____
_____
_____
_____
_____
_____
_____
_____
_____
_____
_____
_____

Character_____Object_____
Scenario_____

_____
_____
_____
_____
_____
_____
_____
_____
_____
_____
_____
_____
_____
_____
_____
_____
_____
_____
_____
_____
_____
_____
_____
_____
_____
_____
_____
_____
_____
_____
_____
_____
_____
_____
_____
_____
_____
_____
_____

Character
Roll 1 Number

1. Lawyer
2. Pickpocket
3. Fry cook
4. Carnival ride operator
5. Opera singer
6. High school dropout

Object
Roll 1 Number

1. Cable box
2. Eyedropper
3. Movie stub
4. Pacifier
5. Flip flop
6. Battery

Word
Roll 1 Number

1. Black
2. Intrigue
3. Analyze
4. Tell-all
5. Home
6. Respond

Character_____

Object _____Word _____

_____
_____
_____
_____
_____
_____
_____
_____
_____
_____
_____
_____
_____
_____
_____
_____
_____
_____
_____
_____
_____
_____
_____
_____
_____
_____
_____
_____
_____
_____
_____
_____
_____
_____
_____

Character_____

Object _____Word _____

_____
_____
_____
_____
_____
_____
_____
_____
_____
_____
_____
_____
_____
_____
_____
_____
_____
_____
_____
_____
_____
_____
_____
_____
_____
_____
_____
_____
_____
_____
_____
_____
_____
_____

Character_____

Object _____Word _____

Character_____

Object _____Word _____

_____
_____
_____
_____
_____
_____
_____
_____
_____
_____
_____
_____
_____
_____
_____
_____
_____
_____
_____
_____
_____
_____
_____
_____
_____
_____
_____
_____
_____
_____
_____
_____
_____
_____
_____
_____

Character_____
Object _____Word _____

_____
_____
_____
_____
_____
_____
_____
_____
_____
_____
_____
_____
_____
_____
_____
_____
_____
_____
_____
_____
_____
_____
_____
_____
_____
_____
_____
_____
_____
_____
_____
_____
_____
_____
_____
_____

STORY BUILDING

Character
Roll 1 Number

1. 4- year-old piano prodigy
2. Skateboarder
3. Court reporter
4. Esthetician
5. Grill master
6. Shell collector

Word
Roll 1 Number

1. Rash
2. Interview
3. Party
4. Smokes
5. Defensive
6. Easy

Scenario
Roll 1 Number

1. Interrupting a thief
2. Cookies burning in an oven
3. Power goes out at a formal function
4. Train hits a car parked on the tracks
5. Blackjack dealer disappears
6. Cashier discovers a counterfeit 100-dollar bill

Character_____Word_____
Scenario_____

_____
_____
_____
_____
_____
_____
_____
_____
_____
_____
_____
_____
_____
_____
_____
_____
_____
_____
_____
_____
_____
_____
_____
_____
_____
_____
_____
_____
_____
_____
_____
_____
_____

Character_____Word_____
Scenario_____

_____
_____
_____
_____
_____
_____
_____
_____
_____
_____
_____
_____
_____
_____
_____
_____
_____
_____
_____
_____
_____
_____
_____
_____
_____
_____
_____
_____
_____
_____
_____
_____
_____
_____
_____
_____
_____

Character_____Word_____
Scenario_____

_____
_____
_____
_____
_____
_____
_____
_____
_____
_____
_____
_____
_____
_____
_____
_____
_____
_____
_____
_____
_____
_____
_____
_____
_____
_____
_____
_____
_____
_____
_____
_____
_____
_____
_____

Character_____Word_____
Scenario_____

_____
_____
_____
_____
_____
_____
_____
_____
_____
_____
_____
_____
_____
_____
_____
_____
_____
_____
_____
_____
_____
_____
_____
_____
_____
_____
_____
_____
_____
_____
_____
_____
_____
_____
_____
_____
_____

Character_____Word_____
Scenario_____

_____
_____
_____
_____
_____
_____
_____
_____
_____
_____
_____
_____
_____
_____
_____
_____
_____
_____
_____
_____
_____
_____
_____
_____
_____
_____
_____
_____
_____
_____
_____
_____
_____
_____

Character
Roll 1 Number

1. Stand-up comedian
2. Machinist
3. Ballistics expert
4. Tax accountant
5. 90-year-old Cuban barber
6. Executor of a will

Mood
Roll 1 Number

1. Disappointed
2. Nervous
3. Giggly
4. Romantic
5. Sneaky
6. Worried

Word
Roll 1 Number

1. Answer
2. Whodunit
3. Melted
4. Satisfaction
5. Tedious
6. Cold

Character_____

Mood_____Word _____

_____
_____
_____
_____
_____
_____
_____
_____
_____
_____
_____
_____
_____
_____
_____
_____
_____
_____
_____
_____
_____
_____
_____
_____
_____
_____
_____
_____
_____
_____
_____
_____
_____

Character_____

Mood_____Word _____

Character_____

Mood_____Word _____

_____
_____
_____
_____
_____
_____
_____
_____
_____
_____
_____
_____
_____
_____
_____
_____
_____
_____
_____
_____
_____
_____
_____
_____
_____
_____
_____
_____
_____
_____
_____
_____
_____
_____

Character_____

Mood_____Word _____

Character_____

Mood_____Word _____

_____
_____
_____
_____
_____
_____
_____
_____
_____
_____
_____
_____
_____
_____
_____
_____
_____
_____
_____
_____
_____
_____
_____
_____
_____
_____
_____
_____
_____
_____
_____
_____
_____
_____
_____

Character
Roll 1 number
Even = MC is alone
Odd = Roll again for a companion

1. Sanitation worker
2. Body builder
3. Dental hygienist
4. Realtor
5. Fashion buyer
6. Nanny

IF the MC is alone, add an object
Roll 1 Number

1. Spoon
2. Wedding ring
3. Arcade game token
4. Necktie
5. Highlighter
6. Gavel

Scenario
Roll 1 Number

1. Barroom fight
2. Boss dies in the middle of a job interview
3. Data starts disappearing from a computer screen
4. Waking with a hangover without having alcohol
5. List of hand-written names beside a future date is found in the back of a library book
6. A clay statue goes missing from an archeological dig

Character(s)_____

Object_____

Scenario_____

_____
_____
_____
_____
_____
_____
_____
_____
_____
_____
_____
_____
_____
_____
_____
_____
_____
_____
_____
_____
_____
_____
_____
_____
_____
_____
_____
_____
_____
_____
_____
_____
_____
_____
_____
_____

Character(s)_____

Object_____

Scenario_____

_____
_____
_____
_____
_____
_____
_____
_____
_____
_____
_____
_____
_____
_____
_____
_____
_____
_____
_____
_____
_____
_____
_____
_____
_____
_____
_____
_____
_____
_____
_____
_____
_____
_____
_____
_____

Character(s)_____

Object_____

Scenario_____

_____
_____
_____
_____
_____
_____
_____
_____
_____
_____
_____
_____
_____
_____
_____
_____
_____
_____
_____
_____
_____
_____
_____
_____
_____
_____
_____
_____
_____
_____
_____
_____
_____
_____

Character(s)_____
Object_____
Scenario_____

_____
_____
_____
_____
_____
_____
_____
_____
_____
_____
_____
_____
_____
_____
_____
_____
_____
_____
_____
_____
_____
_____
_____
_____
_____
_____
_____
_____
_____
_____
_____
_____
_____
_____
_____

Character(s)_____

Object_____

Scenario_____

_____
_____
_____
_____
_____
_____
_____
_____
_____
_____
_____
_____
_____
_____
_____
_____
_____
_____
_____
_____
_____
_____
_____
_____
_____
_____
_____
_____
_____
_____
_____

STORY BUILDING

Character
Roll 1 Number

1. Tour guide
2. Detective
3. Ballerina
4. Hotel pool attendant
5. Altar boy
6. Pizza delivery driver

Trait
Roll 1 Number

1. Fidgety
2. Unlucky
3. Weak
4. Lenient
5. Animated
6. Conceited

Location
Roll 1 Number

1. Ceramics class
2. Driving range
3. Rooftop bar
4. Grocery store checkout
5. Bike path
6. Top of a water slide

Character_____Trait_____
Location_____

_____
_____
_____
_____
_____
_____
_____
_____
_____
_____
_____
_____
_____
_____
_____
_____
_____
_____
_____
_____
_____
_____
_____
_____
_____
_____
_____
_____
_____
_____
_____
_____
_____

Character_____Trait_____
Location_____

_____
_____
_____
_____
_____
_____
_____
_____
_____
_____
_____
_____
_____
_____
_____
_____
_____
_____
_____
_____
_____
_____
_____
_____
_____
_____
_____
_____
_____
_____
_____
_____
_____
_____
_____
_____
_____

Character_____Trait_____
Location_____

_____
_____
_____
_____
_____
_____
_____
_____
_____
_____
_____
_____
_____
_____
_____
_____
_____
_____
_____
_____
_____
_____
_____
_____
_____
_____
_____
_____
_____
_____
_____
_____
_____
_____

Character_____Trait_____
Location_____

_____
_____
_____
_____
_____
_____
_____
_____
_____
_____
_____
_____
_____
_____
_____
_____
_____
_____
_____
_____
_____
_____
_____
_____
_____
_____
_____
_____
_____
_____
_____
_____

Character_____Trait_____
Location_____

_____
_____
_____
_____
_____
_____
_____
_____
_____
_____
_____
_____
_____
_____
_____
_____
_____
_____
_____
_____
_____
_____
_____
_____
_____
_____
_____
_____
_____
_____
_____
_____
_____

STORY BUILDING

Character
Roll 1 Number

1. Bank robber
2. River boat captain
3. Horror writer
4. Sous chef
5. Weightlifter
6. Stamp collector

Object
Roll 1 Number

1. Walkie talkie
2. Bar stool
3. Sticky note
4. Globe
5. Electric bike
6. Magnetic hide-a-key holder

Scenario
Roll 1 Number

1. Hiding in a safe house
2. Stuck in a airplane bathroom
3. Principal doesn't show for parent-teacher night
4. Hairdresser is found with scissors in her neck
5. Listeners thinks they hear a murder over the radio
6. The cashier's headset is hanging out of the drive-thru window

Character_____Object_____
Scenario_____

_____
_____
_____
_____
_____
_____
_____
_____
_____
_____
_____
_____
_____
_____
_____
_____
_____
_____
_____
_____
_____
_____
_____
_____
_____
_____
_____
_____
_____
_____
_____
_____
_____
_____
_____

Character_____Object_____
Scenario_____

_____
_____
_____
_____
_____
_____
_____
_____
_____
_____
_____
_____
_____
_____
_____
_____
_____
_____
_____
_____
_____
_____
_____
_____
_____
_____
_____
_____
_____
_____
_____
_____
_____
_____
_____

Character_____Object_____

Scenario_____

_____

_____

_____

_____

_____

_____

_____

_____

_____

_____

_____

_____

_____

_____

_____

_____

_____

_____

_____

_____

_____

_____

_____

_____

_____

_____

_____

_____

_____

_____

_____

_____

Character_____Object_____
Scenario_____

_____
_____
_____
_____
_____
_____
_____
_____
_____
_____
_____
_____
_____
_____
_____
_____
_____
_____
_____
_____
_____
_____
_____
_____
_____
_____
_____
_____

Character_____Object_____
Scenario_____

_____
_____
_____
_____
_____
_____
_____
_____
_____
_____
_____
_____
_____
_____
_____
_____
_____
_____
_____
_____
_____
_____
_____
_____
_____
_____
_____
_____
_____
_____
_____
_____
_____
_____
_____
_____

CHARACTER BUILDING

Character
Roll 1 Number

1. Soccer player
2. 12-year-old paperboy
3. Birthday party clown
4. Mason
5. Taxi driver
6. Hypnotist

Object
Roll 1 Number

1. Birdbath
2. Nose-ring
3. Knife
4. Work boot
5. Bag of ice
6. Clothesline

Word
Roll 1 Number

1. Secret
2. Pain
3. Circumstance
4. Family
5. Missing
6. Distribution

Character_____

Object _____Word _____

_____
_____
_____
_____
_____
_____
_____
_____
_____
_____
_____
_____
_____
_____
_____
_____
_____
_____
_____
_____
_____
_____
_____
_____
_____
_____
_____
_____
_____
_____

Character_____

Object _____Word _____

_____
_____
_____
_____
_____
_____
_____
_____
_____
_____
_____
_____
_____
_____
_____
_____
_____
_____
_____
_____
_____
_____
_____
_____
_____
_____
_____
_____
_____
_____
_____
_____

Character_____

Object _____Word _____

Character_____

Object _____Word _____

_____
_____
_____
_____
_____
_____
_____
_____
_____
_____
_____
_____
_____
_____
_____
_____
_____
_____
_____
_____
_____
_____
_____
_____
_____
_____
_____
_____
_____
_____
_____
_____
_____
_____

Character_____

Object _____Word _____

_____
_____
_____
_____
_____
_____
_____
_____
_____
_____
_____
_____
_____
_____
_____
_____
_____
_____
_____
_____
_____
_____
_____
_____
_____
_____
_____
_____
_____
_____
_____
_____

STORY BUILDING

Character
Roll 1 Number

1. Chocolate maker
2. Handyman
3. Bus driver
4. 75-year-old woman
5. ER nurse
6. Arsonist

Word
Roll 1 Number

1. Scream
2. Free
3. Evidence
4. Active
5. Crimson
6. Forget

Scenario
Roll 1 Number

1. Delivery man rings the doorbell
2. Light never turns off
3. Idling car at the curb
4. AA meeting speaker starts foaming at the mouth
5. Empty rowboat is found in the middle of a lake
6. Payphone continues to ring on a street corner

Character_____Word_____
Scenario_____

_____
_____
_____
_____
_____
_____
_____
_____
_____
_____
_____
_____
_____
_____
_____
_____
_____
_____
_____
_____
_____
_____
_____
_____
_____
_____
_____
_____
_____
_____
_____
_____
_____
_____
_____
_____
_____

Character_____Word_____
Scenario_____

Character_____Word_____
Scenario_____

Character_____Word_____
Scenario_____

_____
_____
_____
_____
_____
_____
_____
_____
_____
_____
_____
_____
_____
_____
_____
_____
_____
_____
_____
_____
_____
_____
_____
_____
_____
_____
_____
_____
_____
_____
_____
_____
_____
_____
_____

Character_____Word_____
Scenario_____

_____
_____
_____
_____
_____
_____
_____
_____
_____
_____
_____
_____
_____
_____
_____
_____
_____
_____
_____
_____
_____
_____
_____
_____
_____
_____
_____
_____
_____
_____
_____
_____
_____

CHARACTER BUILDING

Character
Roll 1 Number

1. Guardian ad litem
2. Cabinet maker
3. Inn keeper
4. Mechanic
5. Dog walker
6. Book editor

Mood
Roll 1 Number

1. Chatty
2. Bossy
3. Arrogant
4. Weepy
5. Needy
6. Resentful

Word
Roll 1 Number

1. Background
2. Undeniable
3. Descend
4. Rehab
5. Alive
6. Case

Character_____

Mood_____Word _____

Character_____

Mood_____Word _____

Character_____

Mood_____Word _____

Character_____

Mood_____Word _____

Character_____
Mood_____Word _____

_____
_____
_____
_____
_____
_____
_____
_____
_____
_____
_____
_____
_____
_____
_____
_____
_____
_____
_____
_____
_____
_____
_____
_____
_____
_____
_____
_____
_____
_____
_____
_____
_____

STORY BUILDING

Character
Roll 1 number
Even = MC is alone
Odd = Roll again for a companion

1. Parole officer
2. Robbery victim
3. Football player
4. Train conductor
5. Dance instructor
6. Financial analyst

IF the MC is alone, add an object
Roll 1 Number

1. Piggy bank
2. Large deli pickle
3. Cell phone
4. Grocery bag
5. Sewing needle
6. Nickel

Scenario
Roll 1 Number

1. Candlelight vigil
2. Dog is found in a tree-house
3. Holes are discovered in a backyard
4. Roll of film was hidden in a cupboard
5. MC arrives at a deserted event
6. Dry cleaning comes back with the key to a safe deposit box in a pocket

Character(s)_____

Object_____

Scenario_____

_____
_____
_____
_____
_____
_____
_____
_____
_____
_____
_____
_____
_____
_____
_____
_____
_____
_____
_____
_____
_____
_____
_____
_____
_____
_____
_____
_____
_____
_____

Character(s)_____

Object_____

Scenario_____

_____

_____

_____

_____

_____

_____

_____

_____

_____

_____

_____

_____

_____

_____

_____

_____

_____

_____

_____

_____

_____

_____

_____

_____

_____

_____

_____

_____

_____

_____

_____

Character(s)_____

Object_____

Scenario_____

_____
_____
_____
_____
_____
_____
_____
_____
_____
_____
_____
_____
_____
_____
_____
_____
_____
_____
_____
_____
_____
_____
_____
_____
_____
_____
_____
_____
_____
_____
_____
_____
_____
_____

Character(s)_____

Object_____

Scenario_____

_____
_____
_____
_____
_____
_____
_____
_____
_____
_____
_____
_____
_____
_____
_____
_____
_____
_____
_____
_____
_____
_____
_____
_____
_____
_____
_____
_____
_____
_____
_____
_____
_____

Character(s)_____

Object_____

Scenario_____

_____
_____
_____
_____
_____
_____
_____
_____
_____
_____
_____
_____
_____
_____
_____
_____
_____
_____
_____
_____
_____
_____
_____
_____
_____
_____
_____
_____
_____
_____
_____
_____
_____
_____
_____
_____
_____
_____

READY TO TRY A DIFFERENT GENRE?

Check out the other books in the Roll-A-Prompt Writing Journal Series:

Horror

Sci-Fi

Romance

Fantasy

Genre Mashup

Want to get element sets for free? Subscribe to our newsletter and get a one set each month, along with updates on new Roll-A-Prompt Writing Journals, and invitations to join us for live writing prompt sessions. https://BookHip.com/FZHMZA

Made in the USA
Monee, IL
20 December 2020